I0022958

Painfully Silent:

The Unread Pages of Her Life

by leanne anderson

Painfully Silent is a work of fiction, designed to make you think about life issues. Names, characters, places, and incidents are the product of the author's imagination and are used fictitiously. Any resemblance to actual events, locales, or persons, living or dead, is entirely coincidental.

A Righteous And Pure, Inc. Original

No part of this publication may be reproduced in whole or in part, or stored in a retrieval system, or transmitted in any form or by any means, electronic, mechanical, photocopying, recording, or otherwise, without written permission of the publisher. For information regarding permission, please write to Painfully Silent, 95 Broadway, Malverne, NY 11565.

Text copyright © Righteous And Pure, Inc.

Illustrations copyright © Netmix360LLC

Author's Note

Painfully Silent:

The Unread Pages of Her Life

Writing this book took me on a journey. One that would bring me closer to a friend who felt it necessary to share her stories with me. The turmoil and degree of pain carried through the pages are the everyday lives of countless of nameless and faceless individuals, whose stories remain hidden, like their pain, embedded in their souls for eternity. Most have lost hope, and along with it, their self worth.

I'm dedicating this book to ...

my best friend, my husband who
motivated me

my brother who believed in me

a good friend I thought I lost, you're
Uniquely blessed

to the many individuals out there
without a voice

those who know, and do nothing,
now is the time to do something.

U.S. National Domestic Violence Hotline at 1-800-
799-SAFE (7233)

or TTY 1-800-787-3224

Chapter 1

Alone in the darkest corners of my quiet thoughts, the past hours tormented, and overshadowed my tomorrow. My life was turned upside down, and the memories, like my life, was scattered all over the place.

Holding on to what was good brought some comfort, but as the warm tears ran down my face, I was reminded of my today. It flooded me with unfamiliar emotions, sending a darting pain straight to my heart.

"How did it come to this?"

A life envied by so many watching through the tinted glass windows that hid my piteous future. My life came crushing down with vengeance.

I had ignored all the signs, and now I was lost in a world of pretense, blindsided, confused, and left with the broken pieces of my heart in a pool of shame.

If only I took the time to listen, I would have heard the silent cries of the misplaced expressions on his face, or the overbearing attention and, jealousy that were deliberately misconstrued. I should have listened!

Maybe then I would have also heard the whispers of the unspoken words of those before me that seem to drown the room every time I had to leave. Or maybe the flattering phone calls that never seemed too much at the time.

But for now, flashes of my terror played itself over, and over in front my eyes. I didn't want to watch anymore. This feeling lasted longer than I cared for, and there was no escape. Every thought left me weaker than the last. I had lost everything I had, or was about to.

My selfish greed for love set me on a journey that awakened doubts, forcing secrets, and unanswered questions to invade my fairytale.

And just like that, the monster I feared was no longer in the dark closet, or under my bed. Instead, it was lying in wait, right next to me.

I found a truth that moved my world, and drowned my reality. My life started fading away like ashes in the wind. As if the memories in my head were of someone else's life. The warm kisses that meant much, the laughter, and the smiles that filled my heart were all lies I had planted in my dreams to alter my reality.

Sweet lies that once made me happy, ravaged my faith in love. How did I manage to let love take me down this dark path?

In my frantic search for answers, the doorbell rang, and my heart automatically sank in terror.

"Who could that be?"

I jumped to my feet, and immediately made my way to the foyer. I nervously looked through the peephole. Only this time it wasn't him. He didn't come back home pretending he had forgotten something.

Instead it was Mama who made the trip.

"How did she know where to come?"

"How did she know I needed her?"

I slightly regained my composure, before opening the door.

"How you doing baby?" she asked in a concerned voice, trying to hide that judgmental tone as best she can.

"I'm good Mama," I answered, trying not to sound nervous.

"What you doing here Mama?"

"And how you know where I live?"

"C'mon baby, you should know Mama by now," I heard a familiar voice saying as my mind drifted to what lies ahead.

I found myself staring at the person in the crafted mirror we hung in the foyer last Christmas. Hair all messed up, eyes red and swollen, seemed like she was crying for days.

"Is this what I look like?" I asked myself in a whisper.

I sighed, and looked away in disgust.

"Okay Mama," I repeated, trying to ignore the wave of sadness, and fear that drowned my silence as I watched her walking ahead, praying that she wouldn't go into my bedroom.

Alienating the thoughts of what took place a few hours earlier, I drew comfort in Mama's presence; but it wasn't soon after, my thoughts betrayed me again.

My mind started drifting, remembering that hot summer day we had met. I had just gotten out of a relationship, and had sworn off men for good this time.

And him, well I never thought to ask because I wasn't looking. It was after our second date, and way past first base, when I found out he was sort-of-almost out of a relationship. At that point, things were way out of my control.

We had met that faithful day in the summer of 2000, in my second year at college. Young, curious, and in the midst of trying to find myself, I thought I found me in him.

He was everything I wanted, tall, handsome, and successful. A short list that spoke volume to my heart.

I was at the college library studying for the dreadful end of term exams with my roommates. I had quite a lot to study for, being that I always left my studying for last minute. We knew how much was weighing on this study session, so we tried our hardest to stay focused.

We were at it for a while, when we took notice of this guy that obviously wanted to be noticed. I pretended at first not to see him, but his stares, and deliberate attempts for attention sparked my curiosity.

"Is he for real?" Rachel asked annoyingly. Rachel was the smallest one in our group, and probably the entire school, so we named her Tiny.

Her personality was bigger than she was, and so was her mouth.

" Wish he would just stop already! I don't know how he expects us to study with all that damn noise he insists on making. I would walk over there and give him a piece of my mind if I wasn't so scared."

She looked over at him, sizing him up as if ready to fight.

"You see how tall, and big he is," Tiny continued saying, causing the entire table to laugh uncontrollably, provoking an automatic stare of death from the Librarian, bringing our laughter to a screeching halt. Before we had a chance to settle in after the well needed break, I felt the presence of someone standing behind me. And by the look on Tiny's face, there was.

"Excuse me, but I've seen you a few times on campus, and promised myself next time I see you, I will not hesitate to introduce myself."

He managed to get his rehearsed lines out before being verbally attacked by Tiny again, but this time to his face.

"Well, you did more than just introduce yourself, you almost got us thrown out the library. Not to mention interrupted our studies!" exclaimed Tiny.

"But we had a great laugh at your expense, so that makes us even. Right Tiny?"

I had to interject. She was known to go above, and beyond, and I really didn't want it to get to that point.

She saw right through me. I was interested in hearing more from him.

"I'm going to take a five, anyone coming?"

As the rest of the group followed Tiny, I sat glued to my chair as if waiting for a prize that I had won. It was kind of funny and awkward looking him in the eye after all what transpired, so I used my quick-stare routine to try to play it cool.

"Can I get your number?"

"Why?"

"So I can take you out to lunch or dinner. Whichever you prefer."

"Do I look hungry"?

"I'll do all the eating, I promise," he replied with a devious look on his smooth baby face.

"Here is my number, call me when you are."

Smiling and full of confidence, he handed me a paper, gently fondling my fingers all the way to the tip, until I pulled my hands away. I couldn't help but smile, because at that moment, I knew I was going to call him.

Chapter 2

A few days had passed, and I was sitting in my dorm room bored out of my mind, so I decided to give him a call.

"...Sorry, I can't take your call, leave your name..."

I quickly pressed the end button to prevent it from going to the voicemail. An hour later, I tried again.

"...Sorry,"

"Why the hell he gave me his

number for if he never answers his damn phone."

"URGHHH!"

"URGHHH!"

Although my finals were around the corner, I could not bring myself to having another study session. So, since my first choice never answered his phone, I decided to just lie around and be lazy.

"What's on TV?" I quizzed myself while reaching for the remote. At that very moment, my phone rang, startling me. Without looking to see who it was, I answered.

"Hello."

"Hi beautiful," an alluring voice on the other end replied.

"Who is this?"

I looked at my phone to see who it was, but there wasn't a name.

"Can't recognize your prince charming's voice?"

I felt hot and unsure of my response, so I laughed lightly before responding.

"Hi," I answered feeling a bit owed.

"I knew it was you the moment I saw the missed calls. I was extremely busy. Couldn't help it I promise."

"Oh really? Already to busy for me I see."

"Let me make it up to you, pleassseee."

I liked the way he begged.

"O-Okay. What you doing now?"

"N-Nothing. Should I be doing something?"

"Well, now is your chance. How about you take me out to eat, then catch the new flick playing at the cinema down the street?"

"That's a plan! Pick you up in about an hour."

I never expected him to agree on such short notice, but I was nonetheless delighted.

"Great! See you then."

Dinner and a movie didn't sound too bad. And besides, I was all alone on the weekend. I avoided going out with my friends because everyone was coupled up, and with my luck, I was sure to bump into my ex, and his new trophy.

I knew I wasn't searching, but the attention he was willing to give had an effect on me. I secretly wanted more. I wanted someone to make me feel good.

He was my distraction from all the hurt I was carrying around from the neglect, and emotional torture my ex had put me through during our regrettable four month relationship.

Tonight was my night to be pampered, and to be treated like a lady, and my prince charming was going to be the one to do that.

Before I knew it, he was knocking on my door. I was pleasantly surprised when I opened the door. The smell of Old Spice filled the space between us. He handed me flowers and landed a soft kiss on my neck.

It took me just about five minutes, the distance from my door to his car, to be totally taken aback. My eyes followed him like a lion watching its prey.

"This man is perfect," I breathed to myself.

I admired his confidence, and take-charge attitude. Although a bit cocky, he pushed all the right buttons for me that night.

"NO! NO! NO!" I screamed over, and over in my head. Our date was only a few minutes in, and already it was more trouble than I had anticipated.

My brain was on overdrive.

"Is that me falling for this guy so quickly?"

"Damn!"

I felt my insides on fire with desire, and for a minute when he turned and smiled at me, I thought he saw it too.

"Are you hungry?" I heard him ask.

"What did you say?" I asked, attempting to get more time to extinguish the flames that was slowly burning down the facade that masked my true thoughts.

"What are you in the mood for?"

I would be lying if I said food. All I was thinking about was how good he would make me feel. How I wanted him to run his lips all over my back then slowly....

"Are you ok?" I heard just as my thoughts peaked.

"Sure!"

I had to do something. Just as I was about to ask him to stop, I noticed the car slowing down, and then coming to a complete stop.

"Where are we?"

With everything that was going on in my head, I didn't realize how far we had gotten.

"Well, we are at one of my favorite spots," he answered braggingly.

I recognized the place. My ex had brought me there when we first started dating. I suddenly felt hot in a very uncomfortable way. He looked at me, and realized that something was wrong.

"We don't have to go in if you don't want to. Your choice, anywhere you want to go. I really don't mind. I just wanted to see you again," he confessed.

"How about we just go for a drive, and talk?" I responded, looking in the opposite direction of the restaurant.

"A drive right?"

"If that's ok with you?"

He didn't bother to use words to answer; he just looked at me with a big happy smile.

He slowly drove out the restaurant's parking lot, and headed to nowhere. He just kept driving.

It remained silent for a while, until

we passed this store that my friends, and I usually spent our Fridays at, when there was nothing to do.

"Can you believe that Paps is still open?" I heard him say under his breath, as he smiled lightly.

"What you know 'bout Paps?" I asked.

"Paps? Baby girl Paps, and I go way, way back."

Thanks to Paps' corner store, the unnerving silence in the car went out the window, because from then onwards, it was smooth sailing. My guard was down, and I started feeling more, and more comfortable.

He started talking, and surprisingly, I had a lot to say too. I actually started enjoying the evening.

We decided to park on a random street to talk. The bright lights of the incoming cars blinded me a few times while trying to get more comfortable. But in time, not even the blustering lights, or the roaring sounds of the raging motorists stood a chance. I got so comfortable; even my shoes came off.

I hadn't laugh this hard in so long, and having fun with a guy almost seemed new to me. The night went by fast, and before we knew it, it was past midnight. I couldn't believe we spoke for so long, and didn't run out of things to talk about.

I wondered why I had never seen him on campus previously, and he explained that his job brought him to my college. He worked for this celebrity, and was there only to promote a charity event in collaboration with the college. He actually lived about half an hour away.

"Perfect," I thought to myself. "Only half an hour away!"

The more we spoke, the more I was intrigued. A young black man with a plan, no kids, and never had been married. He handled himself with rare confidence and determination. He had me hooked.

As we headed home, I felt anxious, like I was about to let go of something, even if I didn't know what that something was. I didn't want the night to end. He pulled up on my block, and I turned towards him to thank him for a wonderful night, but found myself staring.

His eyes studied mine as I searched his for a connection. My eyes grew wider, and wider in awe, aroused by the unknown that was about to be perfected.

"Goodnight," I said reluctantly, waiting for an invitation to stay longer.

"Goodnight," I heard from the other end, sending my optimism crashing.

He reached for a good night hug, and I leaned in deeper, finding myself lost in his arms, and hypnotized by his scent. He gently stroked my face as he leaned in some more. His eyes lit up with desire, arousing a passion in me that ultimately broke me.

I felt the warmth of his soft lips on mine, and couldn't find my way back to myself. At that moment, I belonged to him. My body failed to follow through with my new resolutions; evoking the desires I fought so hard to stifle earlier.

My hands slipped around him bringing me even closer than before. So close I could feel his hot breath on my chest. With one hand he stroke my face, and the other cupped my femininity as if molding it, admiring every curve.

"I want you," he whispered softly igniting the fire burning inside.

"I want you more," I murmured, pulling him, and squeezing him tighter and closer towards me, as if to engulf his body completely. I wanted him in me. I needed him in me. He slightly took my hands, and led me to his standard. My expectations far exceeded.

My mind was blown away by his natural tenderness and ability to know the limits of my body. I felt the roars of his manhood, and as he finished up with me, I found myself feeling emotions that I had never felt before.

We were motionless; everything around us stopped, except for the morning light seeping through the darkness. A soft smile escaped me thinking about what just took place.

He had his way with me, and I loved every bit of it. Not knowing what to say, I leaned towards him one last time to say goodnight, while quickly pulling my dress over my shoulders.

This time goodnight felt right. He pulled me closer to him as if asking for more. Although flattered, I was way too drained to match that performance, or even come close. So I declined with a smile, and a soft kiss on his receptive lips.

I searched deep within me, and conjured up the strength to walk away. In a helpless surrender, my feet followed, taking me past my friends' rooms straight to mine, undetected. Or so I thought.

Chapter 3

The sound of my roommates woke me up the next morning. I could faintly hear what they were saying, but I was quite sure it was about me. Did they know? I dreaded finding out.

I managed to crawl out of bed, and joined them.

"How was your date last night?" Tiny spared no time asking.

"How did you know I went on a date?"

"Well, I saw when you left, and got into a fancy black truck that I've never seen before by the way!"

"Thought you went out with Jerry last night?"

"Nope, we decided to stay in."

"Okay."

"So are you gonna spill the beans?"

"And did you give it up?"

I almost choked on the orange juice I managed to grab, as I wormed my way past the mob.

"Why the questions, Tiny?"

"I just went out on a date, that's all. Nothing to talk about!"

"Well, your appearance begs to differ. You look torn up like you just came from the club partying all night. And either you like wearing men's cologne or someone was all over you, and maybe all up in you too."

Instead, I turned my back towards her, ignoring her attempts to get me talking.

I wanted to wipe that devious smile she plastered on her face, trying to make me cave in to her demands. I didn't have a story to tell, and I was sticking to that.

My stomach growled both in fear, and in hunger. We never got the chance to eat dinner, and now I was paying for it.

"You must be out your mind Tiny," I laughed, and went back to my room completely losing my appetite again.

I sat on the bed saturated with his scent, staring at the cracks in the ceiling, feeling completely paralyzed. My mind was blank, but fixed on the problem. I didn't know which thoughts to explore.

I started to feel smaller and smaller, when suddenly the thoughts of Bri, a freshman that I had met last year invaded my attempts at finding peace.

Back then, I found her in a bathroom stall crying, because she thought she was pregnant, and the boy responsible didn't want anything to do with her. Story was that she went out with him, had sex on the first date, and the very next day, he supposedly went around saying that she was a slut, and that she had slept with both him, and his best friend that same night.

He didn't care that she was a virgin, and that he was her first ever. In fact, everyone knew it, at least those who mattered, that it was his mission to 'bag' as many virgins as he possibly can before graduation. I guess she never got the memo.

I was stunned to see her in the bathroom stall crying. She was one of the most popular freshmen on the cheerleading team, but after that fiasco, she was known as 'Fast and Easy Bri.'

"Gosh, I don't stand a chance!"

Screaming out softly in my room didn't help much. I felt more, and more ashamed by the minute.

Tiny had rattled up some emotions that caused a chain reaction with all her damn questions. I wasn't sure what to think.

"Am I that one night stand girl, part of the Fast and Easy crew now?"

Maybe Bri and I will become good friends, and someday get a good laugh from all of this.

But that day was no where close,

and I was left thinking...

Chapter 4

I spent the whole day, and the day
after that thinking about him, and
wondered if he was thinking about
me. I wasn't about to call him first. I
figured if he wanted me, he would
call.

The days went by slowly not
hearing from him. I started getting
worried. At first I thought it was
cute playing the who-calls-who first
game, but now it became serious.

I last saw him Friday, it was now

Tuesday.

He plagued my mind the entire time. Even when I was in class, I barely heard what the teacher said.

"Are you okay?" Tiny asked in Economics class, with a worried look on her face.

Her words flew right over my head.

"You need to pay attention girl! You know how Mrs. Dean gets. She will fail you for no reason."

As much as she was right, I couldn't function. I needed to hear from him. As soon as class was done, I hurried to the library to see if I would run into him, but no such luck. The walk to my dorm seemed so much longer than it usually was, until my phone rang.

My heart sank. I wished it was him before I answered.

"Hello," I slowly answered, going against my heartbeat.

"Couldn't stop thinking about you. I need to see you now. Are you up for it?"

Without hesitation, I answered, "Sure, come over!"

I ran all the way to my room to get ready. Before I knew it, he was knocking on my door.

"Told you I couldn't wait," he said smiling as I opened the door.

As he walked past me, he softly touched my face. I felt goose bumps all over. I sat on the couch, and he sat in the front, and leaned back allowing me to embrace him. I held him close to my heart, wondering where he had been all my life. He gently held my face, and kissed me. I kissed him back.

Being in his arms felt good. I felt

safe. Although the desire to connect on another level was bordering with every touch, I felt satisfied in his warm embrace.

It was about seven that evening when we decided to go to the Boardwalk not too far away. The mix of the sea, and the ease of the night would complete a perfect day.

We gathered a blanket, and a few other things, and headed out. The drive was noticeably quiet, however, it was only after arriving there, that I realized that he was a bit bothered by something. I tried to play it off, but it kept tearing me up inside. I had to say something.

"Are you okay?" I asked feeling uneasy.

Silence.

My stomach felt weak, but still full of promise I asked again. This time, he handed me his phone. I looked at him confused.

"What am I looking at?" I asked with a slight elevation in my voice this time.

Silence.

I pressed the power button on his phone only to realize that he had missed more than a few calls, and had even more text messages.

Suddenly I knew. My face sank to the floor. My eyes teary.

"It hurts to see you like this," he said touching my face.

"But I thought I should let you know now rather than later..."

"Let me know what!" I yelled out interrupting him.

"That you actually have someone waiting on you? That you are breaking another girls heart like you're breaking mine now?"

This time I could not control my tears. Embarrassed by my willingness to trust so quickly, I turned away to hide the tears that were rushing down my face.

The memories of my past came to play. I felt dirty, and naked. My heart was again in turmoil. My chest felt tight, and I needed to breathe. I quickly opened the door, and ran straight to the sand. I sat down with my face buried in my hands, still crying.

I heard a door slam behind me, but wouldn't dear look back. I didn't care, and I didn't want to see his face. I was in a familiar place; heart broken, confused, and angry.

Soon after, I felt his touch on my shoulder. Only this time, it was different. His hands were shaking, and cold. Even his voice was shaky when he tried to apologize.

"I'm sorry," he whispered in my ears.

"It was not my intention to hurt you, but you did not give me a chance to explain."

I didn't want to hear him. I wanted to scream at him, while scratching his eyes out. I raised my head and gave him that look that said BACK OFF! But instead he drew closer to me.

"I wanna talk please," he begged. "You don't have to say a word. I'll do all the talking."

I sat in silence, oblivious to my surroundings, even the loud whispers of my bleeding heart persuading me to leave.

"I never intended to hurt you," he said in that shaky voice he first tried to apologize with.

"I was trying to do the right thing, to make you aware of the situation before it got out of control. I didn't think you were going to get all crazy without hearing me out"

"Crazy?" I retaliated immediately from the blows of his piercing words.

"Please, I didn't mean it like that," he pleaded.

"See, this isn't my girlfriend; well not any more anyway, but she refuses to accept that I have moved on. She insists that it will never be over, and we can work through our problems, but I'm not interested in doing that."

I looked up at the perfect moon that was unveiling my tears. The silence made the place eerie. I wasn't sure how to feel. He sat next to me, staring, waiting and hoping for a reaction, any response that would determine his next move.

"Can you not stare at me right now?" I asked still as angry as before.

"I really need you to understand that I'm completely over her. We've tried making up more than I can count, but it always ends the same way. I have been looking for something different, special, and I think I've found it," he said lifting my chin with his finger.

His eyes caught my eyes, and I couldn't be mad at him anymore. He smiled at me with his eyes, and I looked away, pretending to still be angry. I didn't want him to know that being mad at him was like taking my breath away. And that I was already, maybe, in love with him, and it scared me.

We sat quietly next to each other. I could hear the slow blowing breeze as it went by, bringing along the fresh smell of the ocean. The moonlight glistening on the clear blue water brought peace, as the waves elegantly leaped onto the shore, taking with it the debris that lay in its path.

And as the darkness moved in, the stars occupied the sky like a blanket of lights shining brightly, sheltering me.

It was a perfect escape, a perfect beginning, and a perfect time, that was almost overshadowed by confusion. I took a deep breath and inhaled the beauty that surrounded me, waited a little longer, and then exhaled.

I was ready.

I tried my best to understand the situation, and how it was out of his control.

"You can't control the actions of

another person," I told myself.

Besides, he still didn't know how deep my feelings were for him. Maybe if he did, he would run far away. So I waited to tell him.

Chapter 5

As the days became weeks, and weeks became months, the bond between us grew stronger.

I often found myself amazed by how much in tuned he was to my needs then. As time elapsed, our relationship revealed much, but most of the unknown stayed hidden because of his constant gifts, and sweet dangling words.

It almost seemed magical to me, like we shared a secret that belonged

to just us. We had our special
language that only we understood,
and that made me feel unique.

   I felt him in that special place that
remained reserved for him. I
couldn't live without him now that I
had him. I visualized us spending
many nights under the stars, holding
each other's hands while taking
walks in the park.

   I had planned our whole life
together in my head. In the
beginning he went beyond to make
me feel secure, and loved everyday,
showering me with flowers and gifts.
At times he would make silly faces
just to put a smile on my face. He
was my addiction.

   I can still remember the first day
he took me to his house. I thought it
was a big deal then, and thinking
back, I believe the excitement of him
taking that step blinded me from the

silent stares of the emptiness that lived there.

All I saw was a blank canvas for our new start. I convinced myself that I will be the one to make it a home, and so I kept my eyes on the prize.

Getting use to the bare walls was not easy, but I did it knowing that I would sooner than later, add some warmth and love to it.

I remember questioning him about the emptiness, and lack of character in such a beautiful house, but he said that it'd be a home soon. And I smiled.

All the house needed was a woman's touch. Just like I needed his.

When he was gone, I craved his touch like my life depended on it. The way he would hold me, and I would fall asleep in his arms was magical. I counted the days until he came back to me.

I found myself wrapped up in his world, while slowly losing mine.

I hated when he left for days, sometimes weeks, but his job required much of him. Being in that house alone scared me, but I did it for us. He always preferred me being at his house when he was gone. He said it made him feel better knowing that I was there waiting for him to come home. And I would smile.

November of 2000, a few months after we met, was the first time I joined him on a trip. He flew me over first class to be with him on Thanksgiving, since he could not make it back in time. I had planned to be there for only five days, but it was hard leaving him.

The day I had to leave he refused to

take me to the airport, and begged
me to stay. I thought it was cute, so I
eventually caved in. It was the best
two weeks of my life.

I didn't think about how it was
going to affect school, or anything for
that matter. My mother, friends and
professors were furious. Everyone
but us! We were living it up; island
hopping, relaxing on white
sandy beaches, shopping without
limits, making love in five star hotels
without a care in the world.

That was the life I always dreamt
of. I envisioned being happy like
that, not worrying about money or a
dead end job. It was a promise I
made to myself seeing the struggles
my mom had gone through; never
settling until I found what I truly
wanted.

For all the bad relationships with
mediocre treatment and neglect, I

was going to enjoy this one. He was what I wanted, and the perks came with him.

He made me feel important, wanted, and loved. I couldn't imagine being without him, and couldn't figure out how I managed before him.

The night before we flew back home, we went out to dinner to celebrate his success. When we returned to the room, bouquets of orange orchids, and candles filled the room.

As I walked in, he took my purse, and placed it on the end table. He gently undressed me placing a white silk robe on my naked body. He cradled me like a baby in his arms, and took me to the bathroom, where a bath was already drawn. Pink rose petals covered the entire floor.

"I want you to relax, and think

about us. How happy you make me, and how I can make all your dreams come true."

I managed to whisper a faint "I love you," as I tried hard to keep my excitement down. I was happy, totally, and completely happy.

"I'll love you to the end baby," he promised, as he slowly took my robe off.

"I would like to do this every chance I get, only if you give me the opportunity too."

Totally intoxicated by his love, I promised to always be his.

"I'm completely yours! You are all I live for."

Chapter 6

There were many more trips together. Our relationship grew quickly, and spending time with him took priority over everything. My day was overshadowed by his need to see, and feel me; and nights apart were spent on the phone till I fell asleep.

We spent every waking moment together, and it started to show.

My grades suffered, and my friends were no longer in my life. It was just he, and I, and he loved it that way. I slowly lost my identity with every minute I spent with him. The confidence I longed for, I found in him. The security I searched for came in abundance, and blinded me. I ate the things he ate; I loved the things he loved. I loved him.

For a young, talented, smart, and beautiful young lady, I lost the ability to think for myself. For as many warning signs I had unconsciously or maybe purposely ignored, I was about to be rudely awakened.

Chapter 7

"How you doing baby?" Mama's voice asked softly.

"I'm doing great Mama!"

"So why you not calling Mama?"

"No reason Mama."

"Ever since you start seeing this boy, I don't hear from you as often as I use too. Is he trying to keep my baby from me?"

"No Mama, he's not!" I replied almost tired of defending him to her, and her to him.

I guess she heard it in my voice, and changed the topic.

"So how are dem grades?" she asked, not knowing that topic too, was not the best of choice.

He noticed the change in my tone of voice, and that I was irritated by something Mama said. And before I could answer Mama, he snatched the phone from my ears, almost ripping it off.

"What the hell are you saying about me now old witch?"

More concerned about what Mama was about to say to him, I tried to playfully regain control of the conversation by reaching for the phone smiling, but instead, was given a slight push, with a cold stare that instantly wiped the smiles off my face.

"What the hell is wrong with you?" he yelled out, leaving me disarrayed, not knowing whether he was talking to Mama or me.

At that point, I pictured Mama taking off her wig, and bracing herself to curse the Sunday teaching out her soul.

All I heard was screaming from the other end, and he threw the phone to the wall, breaking it in half.

"I'm gonna get you another phone, and I bet she won't get that number." he said, puffing his chest as he walked away.

I looked at him in disbelief, wondering what the hell just happened?

"Baby, wh-what was that about?"

"I'm tired of your mom always talking about me. It's not a secret that she hates me, but I don't care,

I'm not sleeping with her. So you better know which side you're on."

"Whose side I'm on?" I asked, as he walked away.

He didn't even attempt to stop, glance back or answer my question. He just kept right on walking; straight to the pile of papers he had on the kitchen table.

Although we had planned for me to sleep over that night, he decided to drop me off at my dorm because he had lots of work too do, and couldn't do so with so many distractions.

And just like that without any warnings, the invisible cracks started unveiling. My eyes were beginning to open, and it was scary.

After this incident, I found myself daydreaming about us fighting, and breaking up. Always in that order, except that each time it was for something different, but always petty.

We were somewhere new in our relationship. I had dealt with cheating boyfriends before, and even had to deal with controlling ones, but I always managed to leave them without a second thought.

With him, it was different. I felt him under my skin. He had managed to make me believe that I couldn't survive without him.

Something was not right, and I couldn't figure it out.

"Is he having problems at work?"

"Am I not woman enough for him?"

My mind was all over the place looking for reasons, and making excuses for his actions.

I wasn't sure what to think or believe. All I knew was that he wasn't the man I fell in love with. Something changed.

Should I ask him? I wanted to so badly. It would have saved me a lot of worrying, but each question I asked myself; I managed to find a reason not to confront him.

I needed someone to talk to, to steer me in the right direction. Tiny was the only one available to me. She was always a good listener, but I could not stand her advice, no one could.

Everyone who knew her knew that if you couldn't handle the truth, then she wasn't the person to ask. But I was desperate.

I tried to hide the whole truth from Tiny, telling her only what she needed to know, but she saw right through my holes, just like all the other times.

"Are you telling me what really happened?" she asked, seeming unpleasantly sure.

"Yes, Tiny I am," forgetting to mention that he might have slightly pushed me, and I wasn't sure who he yelled at. However, I did tell her that he got upset, and that he had asked me to choose, because he was tired of Mama talking trash about him.

"I'm not going to tell you how to run your life, but you did come to me for advice, so here goes..."

I watched Tiny as she lightly swallowed, snapping her head back to the side. At that point, I knew I was in for it.

"LEAVE THE SON OF A BITCH NOW!"

I stood there waiting, not sure why, but I was ready for her to burst out in laughter, telling me that she was only joking. She loved playing around like that, but the look on her face this time said something different.

She was the least impressed with our relationship, and didn't think he was worth the trouble.

"You are throwing your life away for what? This guy is such a jerk, and I'm surprised you haven't figured that out yet."

She paused for a minute, brushed her hair off her face, and continued.

"I hardly see you at school. You take off for weeks on end, and no one knows where you are, or if you are even alive."

I could see that she was really concerned by the way her voice cracked, and how hard she was trying to breathe easy.

"And your poor mother calls us

every day worried about you, because you cant pick up the damn phone to put her worries to rest with a simple call."

She turned her head away from me, and brushed something off her face again, quickly.

"And now you're telling me it's because of this damn fool you haven't spoken to your mother. What a shame!"

Everything she said went out the door when I heard that my mother had been keeping tabs on me through them.

"Wait! My mother called you guys looking for me? So why no one told me that Mama called?"

"Because she made us promise not to tell you. She is worried sick about you. Everyone is worried sick about you, and that relationship of yours."

I felt a bit betrayed. I had no right to feel that way, but I did.

"If they loved and cared about me then they would understand that I love him. I don't need to explain anything to them, and I sure don't need them."

Chapter 8

Ignoring Tiny's advice was not easy. It echoed in my head, and through the walls in the house every time I was alone.

How come everyone else thought he was bad for me? Was I missing something?

"I know he's not the one to hold a conversation with you if he doesn't like you, and he has a certain mystery about him, but he's just being him."

I thought long and hard about Tiny's words, after my anger subsided.

"Is everyone right about him?" Her words created more doubt than I initially had, and I wanted to find out for myself what was going on. I wanted to know for sure, if my heart made excuses for him, and if in fact he was hiding something. Either way, I wanted answers.

So one day the opportunity presented itself. While waiting on him at his house, I found myself snooping around. I went straight to the little white dresser that was sitting comfortably next to his bed, and opened it. I always wondered what was in there.

On the very top were some papers, and a few receipts. In the mix were some pictures of us. I immediately started feeling guilty for going through his stuff, when out of nowhere a white envelope peeping through the right end corner of the mattress caught my eye.

I rushed to the front door to see if he was anywhere in sight. He wasn't. I went back to the room, and left the door slightly open so I can hear him come in. I sat on the chair holding the envelope, afraid to open it.

"What can be so important that he went through such lengths to hide it from me?"

I opened it slowly. Inside were photos of a girl about my age. She was pretty. I didn't know what to make of it. Photo after photo was of her, until I came across one with them together. She had her arms wrapped around him.

They seemed happy. At the right hand corner, it was dated about two weeks prior.

I literally froze in place with my eyes glued to the photo. My mind wondered trying to make some sense of it.

"Two weeks ago? Was that the trip after that big fight we had, and I didn't hear from him till he came back home?"

"Who is she?"

I tried convincing myself it was a close relative, but something about the way she held on to him didn't feel right.

She was very pretty, with long black hair, and legs to go with it. Her smile seemed contagious, as he smiled back at her looking particularly captivated. I hated her instantly, but I couldn't deny her beauty.

She had that glow that pierced

through the photos, making me feel insecure, and ugly at the same time.

I never heard the front door open, and didn't realize he was standing at the bedroom door, watching. It was only after his scent filled the room that I realized he was there.

I looked up slowly. He stood there casually holding his gym bag on one shoulder, and his cell phone in the opposite hands.

"Who is she?" I asked nervously.

He stood there silent, and I knew it was her.

After so long she was still an issue.

"Is this her? Damn it, I asked you a question, answer me!" I cried out nervously.

"Please tell me I'm over reacting, and she is not the person I think she is."

Without uttering a word, he stepped to me. In that moment I felt like something was about to change. I took a deep breath to prepare myself for what came next, but I never saw that coming.

I felt the pain, before I felt the impact of his fist to the left of my face, then a sharp tug on my hair bringing me to my knees.

"Don't you ever talk to me like that again! And what the hell are you doing going through my things woman?"

Still in shock and pain, I couldn't find words. I couldn't find strength. I couldn't find courage. As he let go of my hair, I feel to the floor, shattered. It felt like death, except I was still breathing, and everything flashed before my eyes. I was no longer whole.

Did this really just happen? I

looked down at my hands, and they were shaking.

I looked up to see his face, and the bleakness of his stare confused me even more. I kept looking, but couldn't recognize the person standing over me.

My chest tightened, and I could feel my heart pounding through my blouse. I stood up, and ran to the bathroom. There, in front the mirror, I stared aimlessly. I couldn't recognize me either. I tried to move my jaw, but couldn't. The physical pain was nothing like I had ever felt before, and the heaviness and confusion in my heart intensified the shock. The blank stare haunted me every time I closed my eyes. I was terrified.

"Are you just about done in there? I need to take a shower baby."

I didn't realize how long I was in

there, and before I could answer, he walked in with his towel wrapped around his waist. He wasn't that monster anymore. I saw a glimpse of familiarity with a thin smile that stretched across his face.

"Want to take a shower with me?" He asked as he kissed the tears off my face.

"I guess so," I replied pushing aside both the sadness, and the pain.

I hated to think about what took place. Thinking about it would just make me scream, and I didn't know what would happen then. So maybe a shower would help.

He stepped into the shower while I was getting undressed. I pushed myself past the hurt and joined him.

"Rub some soap on my back baby!"

I stood behind him, staring. The cold water rushed down his back splashing to the floor. I watched how strong he looked, and how easily it would be for him to strangle me in there.

"Pass me the soap," I answered trying to be okay.

"I have to stop thinking about this," I thought to myself.

I slowly rubbed the soap all over his back. He liked it; he always like when we showered together. When I was done rubbing the soap all over his back, he turned around, and pulled me to him.

I felt a small amount of his strength in his grip. He rubbed his hands all over my body. The same hands he used to hurt me not too long ago, and I flinched. He touched my face, and I flinched. I couldn't help it.

"Everything is okay baby," he said kissing my neck, pressing his stiffened manhood onto me.

"I'm not mad at you anymore," he said while stroking my back.

He did something to me that night. His words pierced my heart, and melted my confidence. I still can't fully explain how he did it, but by the time he was done telling me how much he loved me, I was furious with myself for failing him.

"You want some of this?" he asked feeling me up.

I caved in the moment I felt him slip in. It felt good, and I was good. I felt the tension release from my body, and I was enjoying him. It felt so good; I wanted to enjoy him longer.

By the end of the shower we were all in smiles, and everything looked normal again. The eventful day caught up to us while attempting to

watch television. We fell asleep
without warning.

I was awakened by a shortness of
breath. It was only 2:00 am. My face
was wet from my tears. I couldn't let
it go. The warmth of his body
repulsed me, and I pushed away.

I pictured her all over him, and
how he welcomed her in his arms.
He kissed her softly like he does me.

I saw him undress her, and told her
how beautiful she was. Secretly he
truly wanted to be with her. She was
the one who made him feel whole.

I felt worthless, like I wasn't
enough for him. I couldn't satisfy
him, and that's why he hurt me.

"Why are you with me then?" I
found myself yelling, completely
forgetting where I was.

He stretched out his hands to find
me, to feel my warmth again. I slid

myself closer to him. I didn't want him waking up or hearing my cries; so I stifled them, and embraced him with a heart twisted in fear, and hurt.

I couldn't sleep after that. In my head, I rehearsed the way I would act, and the things I would say to him. When he was sound asleep again, I moved away from him, and sat up in bed, waiting.

He woke up smiling, reaching for me to come closer to him.

Chapter 9

"Will you move in with me?" he asked squinting his eyes, as the light peeping through the curtains blinded him.

I was not prepared for that. I wasn't sure if I had even heard him right.

"What did you say?"

"I want you to move in with me," he repeated in an even warmer voice.

"You spend most of your days here

anyway. I think you should just move in, instead of going back, and forth all the time."

I waited to hear these words for so long. I threw hints every chance I got. Every time he would have to drive me back, and forth to my dorm, I would bring up the idea, but he always remained quiet, pretending not to hear.

Not even that day we had below zero degree temperatures, and the snow was knee high, made him say these words. And now, out of nowhere!

"So what do you think?" he asked again searching for an answer.

Not knowing how to think, or whether or not I felt ok to say how I felt, I agreed.

"Maybe it'll be good for us," I thought.

"I really want us to take that next step," he continued, seeming genuinely happy.

I guess I can be happy. I should be happy. I wanted this for so long, and now I'm getting my wish.

He handed me a brand new cell phone.

"Here, I think you will need this. I will call you when I'm done with work today to come over to help you pack up."

"Thanks, but I'm sure I can manage without you. Besides, I don't have that much stuff to pack up anyway."

Not even I believed I could manage without him.

I reached for the cell phone, and pushed it to the bottom of my pocket book, still in a state of disbelief.

"Don't be foolish!" he answered

quickly.

"The faster you pack your stuff, the faster you move in. I don't want to spend another minute without you here with me."

Driving to my dorm was uncomfortable and quiet. I thought of the friends I was leaving behind, but quickly realized they were already gone. I had not seen or spoken to them for longer than what it took to exchange greetings, except that one time with Tiny.

I was always gone, and when I did come home, it was only for a quick second. Even at school, I never had the time to stay back or walk to the dorms together.

"Things won't change that much," I tried convincing myself.

"I practically lived with him already."

I started feeling better about the move. A smile escaped me as I thought about the fun times we had spent together. I walked to my dorm being sure, until I opened a letter that was pushed under my door. It was from the College. I thought it was the normal scare I had grown accustomed to every couple of months, but this time it wasn't.

I was failing all my classes, and my financial aid was being cut off effective immediately. That meant I had to pay for school on my own. I panicked. I lost control of my breathing for a few minutes, and the joy of moving in with him was pushed aside by the uncertainty of the education I had blatantly taken for granted.

I sat down on the floor right next to the couch where I opened the letter. I wasn't inspired to do anything. I sat down in my misery, contemplating on how to fix this mess I had coming for a long time.

"EFFECTIVE IMMEDIATELY!" I found myself yelling.

"Maybe he will pay my school fees. I know he can afford it."

With little assurance, I pick myself up, and packed my things as planned. Before I knew it, I was done, and waiting.

I reached to the bottom of my bag for my shiny new phone, and wondered whom to call. I really had no one to call. I was truly alone, and I felt alone.

"Nothing a call from Mama couldn't cure," I thought to myself as I hurriedly dialed her number, forgetting the ultimatum he had given me.

"Hello!" The warmest voice answered, lifting the heaviness in my heart.

"Hello Mama!"

"How you doing baby?" she asked sounding as calm as usual.

"So you have a new number I see. I tried calling the old one."

"My phone got lost Mama, so He, I-I mean I got a new one, and was so busy with school, that I forgot to call to give it to you."

"Okay baby, Mama is not upset."

"But I'm good M-Mama, I'm doing really good," I responded trying to hide any shakiness in my voice.

"You know, I know when things aren't right baby, so why you lying to Mama?"

Yep! She really did know, but I couldn't tell her what was going on with school, and that he had hit me, then asked me to move in with him.

If there was one person she disliked on this planet that would be him. She would probably suffer a minor stroke judging from their last conversation. So I held it all inside, and smiled.

"And how's school?" she asked leaping over our conversation to something that would soothe her worries. She had so much faith in me doing great at school.

"Are those grades coming along nicely?"

"Yes, Mama!"

"O-Okay, you know you can always talk to Mama right?" she repeated, reminding me that she is always, and will always be there for me.

"I'll call you if I need you Mama," I said as I quickly hang up, holding back my tears.

Chapter 10

He came right after work like he
promised; maybe a tad bit earlier. It
took him very little time to load the
truck. I stood back looking, thinking
that everything I owned was in the
back of his truck. At that moment I
knew it was real, and there was no
turning back.

He waited for me while I returned
my dorm keys to the office. It was
like taking the walk of shame. Even
when walking back to the truck, I felt
a certain tightness in my chest

looking at him from a distance.

A tightness I had experienced before, but ignored it all together. With each step it got worst, almost collapsing, as I got nearer. I stopped to take a break, to breathe, and find balance.

The truth was that I had lost my bearings all in one day, and the only path I had full control of now was the one I forged in the grass to the office, in an effort to return the keys.

He looked at me smiling. I smiled back, trying to enjoy the moment. In my head I was trying to find the right words to explain my school situation to him.

I thought of what I would say to him, and how I would say it. I played it out in my head, but even in my head I was nervous.

I opened the door to the truck, and

sat down heavily; weighted down by my thoughts.

"What's wrong?" he asked, looking at me briefly before driving off.

As I began to talk, his cell phone rang. I sat there thinking about how perfect the timing was, and that I would not get a chance like that again. However, he picked up right where he left off.

"Are you going to tell me what's wrong?" he asked, the moment he hangs up the phone.

"I can tell that something is bothering you."

"I really don't know where to start or how to say this, but..."

"What is it... you don't want to move in with me?"

"Oh no, that's not it baby! I am really happy we're doing this.

Besides I always dropped you hints, but you never seemed to get them," I said, slightly stroking his thighs reassuring him.

"Anyway, I got a letter from the school informing me that I was no longer going to get financial aid. So basically, I'm out of school because there is no way I can afford the tuition, and I could never put Mama in that position."

I squeezed everything out in one breath. I was afraid that if I stopped, I wouldn't finish, but when I looked up, and my eyes met his, the look on his face frightened me into silence.

A shadow of fear raced before my words, and I got tongue-tied. He looked at me with that blank stare that I feared once.

"What are you talking about?" he asked, exhaling harshly.

"I have to pay my own tuition, because my grades are bad, and have been bad for a while," I murmured shaking hopelessly in the passenger seat.

"Thought you were doing good, first I ever heard of this," was his response, shaking his head in disbelief.

"What happened, couldn't handle the pressure?" he asked grinding his teeth so hard, I could hear it seating beside him.

"With all the traveling, and time spent over at your house, I never had the chance to study, or to make up for missed classes. So I kept falling behind."

"So what are you saying, it's my fault?"

"No baby, that's not what I'm saying at all."

Recognizing the escalation in his voice, I quickly tried to dismiss the conversation in hopes to savor what little pride, and happiness I had left.

We drove home in total silence after that. A silence that was becoming all too familiar between us. In my head, I played it all over again. His reactions, his replies, his questions, his silence, were all closely scrutinized in hope to convince myself that he was not angry.

When we got to the house, we carried all my stuff to the empty room, still in silence.

"I'm thirsty," I called out to him trying to start a dialogue.

I went to the kitchen to get a cold drink of water. He followed. I pour the class of water looking across at him smiling. Between the smile, and reaching for the glass it happened again.

Before the glass could touch my lips, I felt a blow to my head, and fell instantly. The glass survived the fall.

I could hear him yelling. He was so mad it seemed like he had forgotten how to breathe, and was foaming at the mouth.

"I'm sorry, I'm sorry!" I yelled back, not knowing what to say, or how to calm him down.

He fell to the floor beside me after his crazy rant. He sat next to me breathing heavily, and with each breath the anger melted away.

"I'm sorry he whispered," as the last of his anger disappeared, hiding behind his insecurities that his eyes revealed.

He held my face, and kissed me, trying to get back to a place of peace.

"I have no idea what happened. I promise it won't happen again. Will you forgive me baby?"

Blocking out the pain, I answered," I know baby, and I forgive you."

And although I tried to deny it, my heart still loved him deeply, so I blamed myself yet again, for what had taken place.

Chapter 11

For the rest of that day, he had
treated me with some care, and later
that night he held me close, with a
grip that spoke his fears. If only he
knew I had no strength, the will, or
the means to leave him, maybe he
would've slept better.

I lay on his chest unable to sleep,
listening to the irregular thumping of
his heart. It took me back, to a
memory that I had trapped in the
crevasses of my scattered mind. It
was of Mama. What she told me

when I asked her why.

"Why do you allow him to treat you this way, and still love him?" I asked her so many years ago about her love affair with daddy.

She was more than ready to answer. I guess she knew that I wasn't a baby anymore, and that I would one day be curious about what was going on.

"I can tell you this," she answered as she pulled a chair at the kitchen table leaving an open invitation for me to join her.

"When you fall in love, listen to his heart. Listen to see if his beat matches yours," she told me.

With tears running down her tired face, and caught up in an everlasting battle for love, she sighed, and looked me straight in the eye, and said: "If it doesn't, then you're in trouble. You will be caught up in trying to make his heart beat match yours. Once you're hooked, you will do whatever it takes for him to love you, even if it means losing yourself."

She then pointed to my chest. "Ohhh, and you don't wanna know about that pain he can put on you baby girl. You better pray he come correct. Lord knows."

I casted her a confused look.

"But mama," I began, "that doesn't make any sense."

She chuckled, then stopped, and held her chest grimacing. Back then, I thought it was because of chest pains that came with old age, but as I grew, I learnt to tell the difference.

"Love makes no sense. That I agree with, and will bet my last dollar on," she kept saying as she looked outside the small kitchen window pondering on some past memory that seemed to have caught up with her.

Over the years I watched my mother suffer at the hands of the man she loved. With every used tissue, every broken glass, and empty bottle I picked up, I vowed to myself over, and over again, to never make my mother's mistakes.

Her advise carved somewhere in my mind, but still remained questionable.

As a child, I saw my mother go through so much, all in the name of love. She spent her whole life loving against impossible odds; loving a man with two families, with a heart just as divided. Mama knew, but wouldn't do anything about it.

"I was first," she would always say out loud, trying to convince even her own heart from giving up.

I always wondered how my other siblings were like. Would they like me? Do they miss him like Mama, and I do when he's with them? At times I would have to stop myself from thinking too much about it, because I would get really sad.

"I can only imagine how Mama feel," I would say to myself.

My mom was all I had. My dad of-course kept coming, and going. Mostly going! That was typical in almost every household in our town.

Daddy would be gone for months. One time he was gone for over a year. But when he came back, Mama welcomed him with open arms. I had seen them at their best, and I had seen them at their worst.

She had suffered so much loving this man, yet she could not leave him. When he was gone, she was miserable. She was physically sick.

I'm not saying she was a weak woman, because she is one of the strongest women I know. I've seen her triumph over so much, and made life possible for us with so little.

But Daddy, he was her kryptonite, and he knew it. I always wondered how they lasted as long as they did. But as I grew up, and the years passed by, I realized that their love, what they shared, was constant, and never changing. It was the love she had grown accustomed too, and the only love she knew.

The entire block knew them. When they argued, everyone heard. You could hear them as far as Mr. Joe's corner store, which was two blocks down from Mama's house.

I remember the last time I saw daddy and Mama together, they were arguing, then made up, and I'm pretty sure they argued after that. It was a Saturday afternoon, no different from any other, except for the quiet noise that filled the house on returning from a trip to the grocery store.

Mama had sent me to get some sugar, but I knew we didn't need it, because she had sent me two days prior to buy some when they were arguing. Trips like these were spent with my best friend Mary. We would talk for a while before I agreed it was safe to go back home. By then they would have solved their problems, and the house would be filled with laughter again.

On that particular day, I walked pass the living room, and entered the kitchen where I found my mom sitting at the table holding her head down. She had been crying. Mama only cries for daddy.

I looked at her, with tears in my

eyes, already thinking of how we were going to pick up the pieces again.

"How long are you going to do this Mama?" I asked, full of both sadness, and anger.

I hated what she allowed daddy to do to her, and I hated daddy for doing it.

I sat next to her trying to comfort her, stroking her back. Her frail body confirmed that she was not as young as she use to be. Her hair fell to her back with hints of grey reminding me of the hard years past, and wondered how much more she can really endure.

Mama met daddy when she was only fifteen. He pursued her intensely. She never stood a chance with his charm, and sweet-talking.

Back in the day, daddy was "The

Man". All the girls wanted him, and all the boys wanted to be him. So I guess Mama felt flattered that he chose her, and how every girl wanted to be her.

"Are you going to be OK?" I asked knowingly.

She raised her head, and I saw that same sad, and pathetic look I had seen a million times before.

"You got to let him go Mama, or he is going to be the death of you?"

She burst out crying holding on to the sleeves of my shirt. Things had been good for almost three months, the longest he had ever stuck around. I got use to seeing him around the house, and Mama, poor Mama, thought he was gonna stay for good this time.

We started bonding as a family, and Mama was happy, the happiest I'd seen her in a long, long time. So I knew it crushed her heart seeing him walk away after what she thought was going to be a new start for us.

I continued rubbing her back, and playing with her hair. She always loved it when I did that, but it didn't seem to make her feel better. She was hurting, and I couldn't do anything about it.

Just like I couldn't do anything about my school situation. I really wanted to go back. I was so close to finishing, and Mama, she would die if I didn't.

She was so proud of me when we found out that I was going to college.

"Nothing good comes out of these parts," she would say to me everyday.

"You better make something of yourself. I'm working my ass off to send you to this fancy school so you can have a chance."

Mama always said she wanted more for me, so she never stopped until she got me into this private school, two bus rides, and a couple of train stops away. But I didn't mind the travel. I learnt so much along the way. It was beautiful, and I loved it there. It made me forget where I was from.

Where I grew up, there was really nothing much to offer, except dead end jobs working in the factories, and mediocre schools that have yet to produce one college bound student.

Except for Mary of course, who made it to community college two towns over. But that still doesn't count, because she had her cousin from her daddy side of the family tutoring her on Sundays when she would visit for church.

"Oh how I wish Mama was here right now. She would know how to put the pieces together. She was good at sorting my life out."

Chapter 12

With a wish in my heart, I finally feel asleep. I could feel the cool air blowing through my hair, and the softness of its touch on my face.

Strangely, I hear birds singing in the distance, and as the sun filled me up, I felt the depth of my pain on the inside intensify. I looked down, and there was no end.

I looked back, and could see my mother reaching out to me. Her face wet with tears, her stomach hallow.

I heard the rumors of a girl who

seemed to have it all, then I saw faces laughing and fingers pointing, jeering at me. Tired, wanting it all to end, I thought of how easy it would be to let go. I thought of the pain, and how it would be no more.

But as I drifted further, and further, a voice pulled me back in. I recognized the voice. I recognized the dreams that it spoke of. They were mine.

I was waiting on love to rescue me, but the wait was long, costly, and painful. The tears came streaming down, and I could no longer remain still. I felt my chest crushing taking my breath away, slowly.

"Mama! Mama!" I yelled out.

My scream resounded through the hollow walls escaping to the trees outside.

My eyes still clouded with tears, I

managed to open them slightly
realizing we both had fallen asleep,
and he seemed to have found a
comfortable spot on my chest. He
awakened with tears in his eyes too.
It looked like he too had a bad dream.

"Why you cheating on me bitch?"
he yelled when our eyes met.
"Why?"

He reached for my throat,
wrapping his large muscular hands
around it. I was scared.

He glanced down at me from the
corner of his eyes, and I could see
death. I wasn't ready to die.

With a furious cry, and a final push,
I finally got him off me. His eyes
were blank, and his stare was cold.
It was as if he didn't even know that
he was choking me.

It didn't take much for him to hurt
me, and there was nothing I could do

to stop him.

And I was again afraid...

I had watched my mother swallow
her pride, and did unquestionable
things in the name of "LOVE" and so I
did what I learnt.

To keep my sanity, I spoke with my
pen. I kept a diary. In there, the
truth lay, coded in my now secret
language, that only I could
understand.

Was I becoming my mother?

Chapter 13

Time went by slowly from then on, most times painfully. He did unspeakable things to me.

Things I wouldn't dare write in my diary. Writing it meant that I had to relive it. Like the time he beat me so badly, I stayed in the same spot for two days, only to be awaken by the stench, and wetness of his urine all over my face.

On days like these, I had to dig a bit deeper to keep my head above my shoulders.

We had bad days, and not so bad
days. On a not so bad day, he would
take me out, have a few drinks, and
retire after a lengthy night of sex.
Sex managed to calm things down
for a few.

Even on days when sex felt more
like a punishment than pleasure, I
found comfort knowing that it would
bring me a few hours of peace, if not
a day or two. Giving him what he
wanted, and how he wanted it, gave
me temporary peace.

The not so bad days brought me
through much. My sanity depended
on them, for our bad days were
exceedingly much. One bad day led
to the next, sometimes lasting long
enough to break me, but short
enough to keep me holding on.

I never knew what to say or how to
say things to him. I felt like I was
walking on eggshells every second

spent with him.

His bad days were my worst days. The days when he seemed to blank out, and emerge as this separate entity, programmed to destroy every speck of hope, and laughter in me.

There were days when I would call out for help; I would call out for Mama hysterically, but she never came.

I was trapped in his bad days, enticed by the profound warmth, and sweet caresses of his good days. The bittersweet taste of his kisses was sometimes laced with hope for better days, as I struggled to hold on to each day as it passed by.

I never knew what to expect, with my only weapon being the knowledge of his predictably unpredictable days. I stayed vigilant. Even in his sleep, I lay watching.

I would think back to the simple days of loving him freely. The days I would marvel at his ability to make me smile from within. How he would hold me tight, and protect me from my fears.

All I had now were memories, with a vacancy for a hero to come rescue me.

Chapter 14

Some days I had trouble holding on.
I found myself contemplating
suicide, but Mama's voice always
brought me through. I was once so
alive, full of dreams, and loving life.
Now, my heart was replaced with an
empty black hole that consumed me
each day, burying my hopes
underneath my pain.

I learnt to conceal the pain and
anger perfectly, like a well-trained
animal. Maybe I would open my

eyes, and realize it was just a really bad dream. Maybe, but with each day, my reality prevailed.

I had grown accustom to the physical pain, that it became acceptable, but seeing him smile, and flirt around with other women, broke my spirit in a whole different way.

He was cheating, and the thought made me weaker, knowing that they were enjoying a part of him I use to enjoy.

We were past that place, and I was beginning to accept it, but whenever I saw him touching another woman like he use to touch me, it enraged me.

It created an abnormal escalation of anger mixed with self-pity, occasionally digging me deeper and deeper into depression.

Even at my lowest, he had

managed to break me even further.

So that afternoon when I saw her outside the house, nothing moved except the sleeping rage in me that could no longer be kept hidden with shallow smiles, and false hope.

I had recognized her instantly. She was the one in the photo, the same one that haunted my dreams, and derailed my happiness. She was there from the beginning.

She was standing next to the driveway. She looked as pretty as she did in the photos back then. She stood tall, and strong, sure of herself, and why she was standing there.

The longer I stared, the less anything made sense. In the still of the silence, every thought that crossed my mind was tainted by what seemed to be the truth.

Why was she here? How did she

know where we lived? I felt my heart burning with the pain of unanswered questions that lay heavy, and sinking.

"There you are," said a voice I wished I hadn't recognized.

His voice sounded calm, and sincere. I wished his voice sounded less polite like it usually did addressing me. I wished he had screamed at her, and asked her what the hell she was doing here.

I hated seeing her smile like I use too. Why was she so happy? Did she know of the monster that lay beside me every night?

With eyes peering through the openings in the curtains, I watched as he hugged her. It felt like one of those nightmares I had almost every night when we first started dating. I would wake up with tears streaming down my face, and a shortness of breath. I dreamt of him choosing her, telling her that she is the one.

The thoughts of him with her had stained my conscience, and I couldn't look away. I wanted to read her body language to see if we spoke that same language, but we didn't.

As much as it was killing me to watch, I waited until she left, then turned, and walked away. For a moment I thought I would just keep walking. Walk through the house out the back door, away from him.

Instead, I waited for him next to the bathroom door. When he came in and saw me, he looked at me knowing. I didn't look vulnerable, and he didn't see tears streaming down my face. I stood tall next to the bathroom door.

That never stopped him before, but the look on his face was priceless. I saw a little fear in his eyes. Just a little, but enough to make him think twice about his next step.

I recognized that look of fear - I lived it. He was uneasy, and shaky. It was that look I drew strength from.

I convinced myself that I wasn't falling to the floor this time. I really didn't know how not too, so I braced myself for whatever as he approached me.

I felt his rage, and anger in his blow. His knuckles were hard, and bulging. My eyes pulsated on impact; my mouth bloodied. This time he didn't care if he left a mark, and it scared me a little, but I stood tall.

"I hope she is worth it," I cried out, wiping the blood off my lips trying my best not to add to the pain.

"Worth it?"

"Worth it?"

He angrily repeated.

"Bitch, you better not say another word before I make it your last!"

Chapter 15

As I watched him walk away, I slowly began to realize that the past few months of holding on, and suppressing my anger, and pain, were in fact transforming me.

The very thing that broke me, ultimately made me stronger indeed.

I heard that saying so many times before, but only at that moment, it truly had meaning.

I picked up my shoulders, and stood tall like I promised. I walked pass the mess, stepped over the broken lamp, and went to wash the now nauseating stench of Old Spice off my body.

When I got out the shower, the house was quiet. He had left. I looked at the mess he had made for a second time. It was more than usual. I walked right through it, and headed for the bed.

I sat at the edge looking outside the huge window that was normally heavily draped blocking the light. The bright sunlight filled the room consuming every corner. I sat there thinking, staring outside almost jealous of the beauty I could not enjoy.

The trees were swaying harmoniously to the sweet mellifluous sounds of the silent wind. It distracted me for a while, but I didn't mind. I thought how nice it would be to feel free like they were.

To dance in the wind without the cares of a world that grew cold around me.

I opened the windows, and paused for a moment to feel the comfort of the soft breeze on my naked body. It felt nice.

"Maybe I can sway like them," I thought.

Surprising to me, the whispers of the wind came blowing wisdom, and change. I felt a stinging sensation in my nipples, and looking down, it seemed to have doubled in size, frozen.

The silence that dominated my days had again showed up. I sat still in all my nakedness. Even my heart stopped beating for a second.

I touched them, and it stung a bit. I cupped my breast, and they too responded. They had grown in size.

How had I not noticed? I remember missing a month...

Thinking back, two months had gone by since my menstrual cycle went off the grid. I thought it was because of all the stress, but to think!

"Is there life growing inside me?"

I rushed to the mirror looking for signs, anything that would indicate that there was a little person growing in me. The close examination of my body revealed nothing. I was as flat as the day I was born, and I felt no different.

I pushed the idea aside. "There's no way I can be. God wouldn't give me that burden knowing what I'm going through!"

"I can't be!"

"I can't possibly be!"

"What kind of life will I be able to give this child," I thought to myself.

As hard as I kept trying to fight the idea, I had to know for sure. I quickly got dressed, and made my way to the closest pharmacy. I didn't care that it was at least a thirty-minute walk or that he may return, and not find me.

Any other day I would be scared to death to even leave the house without his permission, but today, I had a greater fear.

I ran all the way there, and back with enough time to spare. He was still out.

Not wanting to spend another minute thinking about it, I read the instructions, and without delay peed on the stick.

"I'm actually peeing on this stick!"

Who would have thought I would be

in this predicament? I had big dreams for Mama and myself. Thought I would conquer the world. Now I'm in this bathroom, scared, and in pain from beatings that should have claimed my life on many occasions, waiting for results that could further complicate my life.

I couldn't help but think of how pathetic my life was, and that maybe I was about to bring this little person into a world that I'm petrified of.

"How am I going to protect her, if I can't even protect myself?"

Yes, my thoughts lead me to believe that the baby was a girl, and in the three minutes waiting for the results, her life flashed before my eyes. I thought of how scared she would be, and how she would resent me for bringing her into my pitiful world.

I thought of Mama's life, and now

mine.

"She's right!" I started to think about how I was now living Mama's life, and that she would one day live mine.

Distressed, and emotionally drained, I started crying looking at the results in my hand.

I had already managed to ruin her life. I saw her sad face looking up at me, and I was heartbroken. I endured a lot of pain, heartaches, and abuse, but nothing exceeded the hurt I felt at that very moment picturing the despair in her eyes.

It was as if I had pierced my own heart with a knife, and was watching it bleed out.

Chapter 16

A new chapter of my life started after those three minutes. I am now two, with a common threat. Not for a second I thought of telling him. I had to process it all first.

I knew if he knew, he would find a way to blame me, and I would have to pay for it.

While trying to compose myself, I heard the front door open. It was him.

"Still in that damn bathroom?" he yelled out.

"Back so soon? Didn't realize how the time flew by so quickly!" I replied, keeping my calm in check.

He stumbled hearing that quick response, and the fact that I answered all together. I could smell the entire bar on him. The mix of alcohol, and cigarette almost made me vomit. He stood there looking at me with those suspicious eyes.

"What's wrong with you?"

As if I didn't have a thousand reasons to feel sick, and pained up, I smiled.

"Nothing, nothing at all," I replied looking down, and away from him so he couldn't see through my lie.

I walked out the bathroom door, and he walked right in after me. The smell once again moved my stomach, and this time I could not hold it in. I rushed back in, and buried my face in the toilet bowl.

Now more convinced than ever, he stood over me ignoring the stench, and sight, demanding me to tell him what was going on. I knew he already realized it, but was maybe waiting for me to prove his suspicions wrong.

I looked up not knowing what to say.

"Are you pregnant girl?"

My heart raced.

"I asked a question!" he yelled, still hoping to be wrong. I saw his anger escalate with each attempt to breathe, and I saw that blank look.

I shielded my stomach instinctively. In that moment I loved her. I didn't know what she looked like, but I loved her. I was going to protect her.

The blank stares always came first, followed by kicks, and punches, sometimes choking. This time was no different; he came twice as hard, and yelled twice as much.

"Why the hell you got yourself pregnant bitch?"

I silently endured his beatings, and harsh words. Not wanting to do or say the wrong thing to push him even further off the edge, I lay curled up in a ball as much as I could so he wouldn't get to hurt my baby. I silently wept for her, gaining strength from her existence; knowing I had someone to protect.

After nonstop kicking, and punching, he abruptly stopped. I guess he grew tired. He leaned against the wall holding his head. I remained motionless, taking short breaths.

Chapter 17

I woke up the next morning still curled up in a ball, holding my stomach. He was sitting on the chair across the room looking. I had no idea when, or how I feel asleep, but I was happy to be alive.

His uncomfortable stares wouldn't let me do or say much, so I stared back.

"What are we going to do about this problem?" he asked in an unsettling voice.

I knew what he was implying with

his question, but my heart wouldn't let me answer. I couldn't imagine doing that. I had grown so attached in such a short space of time.

It wasn't a surprise that he wanted me to have an abortion, and even less surprised when he demanded that I deal with it ASAP.

"Listen!" he yelled.

"Money is on the dresser, take care of this. I don't wana have this conversation, or this problem when I get back home."

I watched him, as he got dressed, to the very last step out the house. He left behind the scent of Old Spice that almost made me sick to my stomach again. I stood up in all my confusion, wondering what to do.

"Why God Why?" I yelled out feeling trapped by my circumstances.

My emotions spilled outwards, and I couldn't stop my heart from crying. I was so tired of it all. Every waking moment of my life was controlled by this man.

"No more!" I said to myself, shaking my head, attempting to restore the faith I once had in myself.

"I am going to have this child, and I'm going to love her with everything."

I was going to leave him at any cost. My mind was made up. I was sure that I wasn't going to spend another night trapped.

I thought of packing up my stuff, and leaving right away, but how far would I get. I had no car, and no money of my own, except for what he left for me to have the abortion.

"It gotta be tonight," I kept

reminding myself, pasting back, and forth in the room. It felt like a now or never situation, and my chances of success lessen with each second that past, and I did nothing.

I took the money, my passport, and the little valuables I had, and placed it in a zip lock, and hid it in the hamper. The chance of him looking through the hamper was slim to none. I quickly tidied up, got dressed, and left the house.

I needed to go somewhere to kill time, and to clear my head, so I went to the library where it all started. I sat there thinking how different my life would be if I had never met him. And I hated him again.

It had been hours since I left the house, and the scent of Old Spice still lingered. His voice rang in my head over, and over, causing me to hyperventilate more than a few times that day. I wanted him gone, to disappear from my life forever.

I grabbed my bag, and rushed out the library looking for a taxi. I couldn't let him see me walking home after my "abortion".

I thought of a way to end this nightmare once and for all. My sleeping pills would do the trick, I was sure of that. Besides, that was the best plan I had.

Most sleepless nights, when the pain was intolerable, and the flashbacks were overbearing, I used the sleeping pills to evade the present. I had gotten them from this guy who hung out at Paps' corner store a while back. It was earlier in our relationship when the beatings started, and my nightmares were real. All I wanted to do was zone out of my reality, even for a short time. It helped. It did just what was promised, and all it took was one pill.

"Maybe two will do the trick I thought!"

By the time I pulled up in the taxi, I had it all figured out. I entered the house feeling confident. I played the part of being in pain effortlessly, thanks to his help.

"So back to business?" he asked with a grin on his face. Mine was on the inside.

"Can I get something to eat?" he selfishly asked.

He played right into my trap. This man was so predictable, and that was my strength.

"Sure I replied."

Chapter 18

I sat across the table watching him eat. Everything about him repulsed me. The way he held the fork, gently parting his food contradicted his nature.

"Are you going to eat?" he asked, as if concerned.

"You're going to need your strength you know."

Boy was he right. I nodded my head, and reached for the fork holding back the anxiety to please my thoughts.

I watched him put the last bite in his mouth, while slowly reaching for the tall glass of lemonade to his right. He swallowed every drop before letting out a loud disgusting burp.

He sat there feeling content rubbing his stomach.

"I don't ever want to have that problem again," he managed to let out right after another disgusting burp; this time, pushing around the acidic smell of his dinner.

I gagged, and he looked at me funny.

"You did take care of that shit right?" he asked with wondering eyes piercing my stomach.

"Yes, I did," was my only response.

"You want another glass of juice?" I asked feeling a bit disappointed that the drugs had not kicked in as yet.

"Sure," he answered.

"And put some ice cubes in there," he called out as I made my way to the kitchen.

I didn't mind getting him the juice. In fact, I was hoping that he would ask for more, so I simply pushed the request along.

The pills, for some reason was not working as fast as I wanted it to, so I needed to make another batch to secure my plan.

I quickly poured the juice adding the ice cubes he requested, along with two more crushed pills.

"This better work," I quietly reprimanded my plan, stirring the mixture to hide all traces.

I couldn't reach the room fast enough. He grabbed the glass from my hand almost spilling it.

He was almost half way through the glass when he abruptly stopped.

"This tastes different!" he said looking to the bottom of the glass.

"What the hell is this?"

He inspected the glass with a rush.

"What the hell is this?" I heard him yell again, pointing to the bottom of the glass.

As I closely examined it for myself, I spotted some white substance bunched up in the bottom left corner of the glass. My heart started pounding loudly in my ears.

"You trying to kill me Bitch?"

Panting rather violently, he rushed towards me with the glass raised above his head. He swung for my head, and missed. I ran to the room screaming.

At that moment, I knew it was

really my last night there. He was going to kill me. Realizing the room was a bad choice; I attempted to run out the room, but fell right at the door, tripping over his damn shoes.

He caught up quick, dragging me by the leg back to the room. He didn't waste anytime punching, and kicking me all over my body. His rage was beyond reasoning.

He grabbed me by my arm, and turned me over to lie on my back.

"I want my face to be the last you see as I drain the life out your body bitch!" he said softly as he grabbed my throat, squeezing it, tighter, and tighter.

I tried to push him off, but he wouldn't budge.

"Make it easy on yourself, and stop moving."

I couldn't just lie down, and do

nothing. I had one more fight in me I thought. I reached for his manhood, and started squeezing the life out of it. With one had still wrapped around my throat, he managed to get the other loose, and punched me in the stomach.

"My baby, please don't kill my baby!" I said with the little breath left in me. I couldn't help but plead for her life.

Within that same space of time, I saw his face sink in fear. As faint as my words were, he had heard them. His eyes lit up, and I knew he knew. He had recognized my plan. His epiphany paralyzed him, enabling me to grab hold of a nearby vase, smashing it to his head.

He collapsed on top of me, trapping me under his sweaty mass.

"Get off me!" I yelled, pushing as hard as I can, pulling myself from under him.

He lay there not moving. I stood above him for the first time, looking at the monster that dominated my life with fear, and pain. He couldn't hurt me anymore. I was sure he was dead.

I sat at the edge of the bed. This time I wasn't crying, I wasn't scared. I couldn't feel anything. And as the night went by slowly, and the light piercing through the curtains started exposing me, my mind entered a state of disbelief.

...and alone in the

darkest...

About The Author

Leanne Anderson was born on the small

Caribbean Island of Saint Lucia. She now lives
in Long Island, New York. She has a unique
love for the mysteries of life, and the emotions
that make us uniquely us. After gaining her
Masters of Science in Education, she decided to
embark on this journey; one that led her to
writing. Her love for writing has since guided
her to a heart felt task for discovering the true
nature of the beautiful chaos we call life.

Domestic Violence and Abuse

Domestic violence and abuse can happen to anyone, yet the problem is often overlooked, excused, or denied. This is especially true when the abuse is psychological, rather than physical. Noticing and acknowledging the signs of an abusive relationship is the first step to ending it. No one should live in fear of the person they love. If you recognize yourself or someone you know in the following warning signs and descriptions of abuse, reach out. There is help available.

Women don't have to live in fear:

- **In the US:** Call the National Domestic Violence Hotline at 1-800-799-7233 (SAFE).

- **UK:** call Women's Aid at 0808 2000 247.

- **Australia:** call 1800RESPECT at 1800 737 732.

- **Worldwide:** visit International Directory of Domestic Violence Agencies for a global list of helplines and crisis centers

Male victims of abuse can call:

- **U.S. and Canada:** The Domestic Abuse Helpline for Men & Women

- **UK:** ManKind Initiative

- **Australia:** One in Three Campaign

Content **on this page** was taken from:
http://www.helpguide.org/articles/abuse/domestic-violence-and-abuse.htm

www.ingramcontent.com/pod-product-compliance
Lightning Source LLC
Chambersburg PA
CBHW052135270326
41930CB00012B/2890